MAE C. JEMISON

BY MEEG PINCUS

ILLUSTRATED BY ELENA BIA

WOMEN IN SCIENCE & TECHNOLOGY

 Rourke™

BEFORE AND DURING READING ACTIVITIES

Before Reading: *Building Background Knowledge and Vocabulary*

Building background knowledge can help children process new information and build upon what they already know. Before reading a book, it is important to tap into what children already know about the topic. This will help them develop their vocabulary and increase their reading comprehension.

Questions and Activities to Build Background Knowledge:

1. Look at the front cover of the book and read the title. What do you think this book will be about?
2. What do you already know about this topic?
3. Take a book walk and skim the pages. Look at the table of contents, photographs, captions, and bold words. Did these text features give you any information or predictions about what you will read in this book?

Vocabulary: *Vocabulary Is Key to Reading Comprehension*

Use the following directions to prompt a conversation about each word.

- Read the vocabulary words.
- What comes to mind when you see each word?
- What do you think each word means?

Vocabulary Words:
- applied
- engineer
- experiments
- gravity
- planetarium
- professor
- technology
- volunteered

During Reading: *Reading for Meaning and Understanding*

To achieve deep comprehension of a book, children are encouraged to use close reading strategies. During reading, it is important to have children stop and make connections. These connections result in deeper analysis and understanding of a book.

Close Reading a Text

During reading, have children stop and talk about the following:

- Any confusing parts
- Any unknown words
- Text to text, text to self, text to world connections
- The main idea in each chapter or heading

Encourage children to use context clues to determine the meaning of any unknown words. These strategies will help children learn to analyze the text more thoroughly as they read.

When you are finished reading this book, turn to the next-to-last page for **Text-Dependent Questions** and an **Extension Activity**.

TABLE OF CONTENTS

BIG DREAMS

Mae C. Jemison was born in 1956. Times were different then. Women and people of color had few jobs to pick from. Nobody had been to space yet.

But, Mae dreamed big dreams. She dreamed of space.

"I was a young girl who loved to stare up at the stars," Mae said. "I imagined myself going there."

First Space Place

Mae grew up in Chicago. Her family liked to visit the Adler Planetarium. It was the first **planetarium** in the United States. Mae learned about space there.

Mae loved to read science books and play outside. She loved *Star Trek*, a TV show set in space. She also loved to dance and make art. Her parents loved her curiosity.

In kindergarten, Mae told her teacher she wanted to be a scientist. The teacher asked if she meant a nurse. **"No, I mean a scientist!"** Mae said. She studied hard to become one.

Mae went to high school at age 12. She went to Stanford University to study science at age 16.

She was the youngest student in her college classes. Sometimes, she was the only female. Sometimes, she was the only person of color.

But, Mae got top grades. She led her own dance show. She also led the Black Student Union. Her big dreams felt possible.

Mae's Favorite Science
Mae studied to be a scientist called an **engineer**. Engineers want to know why and how things work. They think up new things and build them.

DOCTOR, DANCER, ASTRONAUT

After college, Mae wanted to be a doctor or a dancer. So, she did both! She became a doctor with a dance studio at home.

Mae **volunteered** as a doctor in Africa for two years. She had to use old **technology** to treat sick people. She dreamed of bringing them new technology.

But, Mae kept thinking about her old dream. **"I wanted to go into space,"** she said. NASA (the National Aeronautics and Space Administration) is where all astronauts in the United States train to go into space. Mae **applied** to be a NASA astronaut.

Going to space is risky. This did not stop Mae. She wanted to try.

GOING TO SPACE!

NASA picked 15 people out of 2,000 applicants. Mae was one of them. Her dream was coming true. She would train to be the first African-American woman astronaut!

Mae trained for five years. She learned how to move without **gravity**. She learned how to fly a jet and a space shuttle. She learned how to parachute and scuba dive. And, she learned more science and math.

Finally, it was time for her to go to space.

Mae went to space with six other astronauts. One was the first Japanese astronaut in space. Two others were the first married astronauts. They flew on the space shuttle Endeavour.

Mae took with her a poster, a flag, and a statue, all representing women of color. **"I thought it was important,"** Mae said. She wanted all people to feel included.

From space, Mae looked back and saw Earth. She saw her hometown. Mae felt small. She also felt a part of everything.

Mae spent eight days in space. She traveled more than three million miles (almost five million kilometers).

Mae did science **experiments** on the space shuttle. She studied frogs and motion sickness.

The country cheered when Endeavour landed safely.

Mae loved being an astronaut. She got to be the first real astronaut to appear on *Star Trek*!

People were surprised when she left NASA. But Mae wanted to follow a dream that began when she was a doctor in Africa. She started a company to bring technology to places in need.

Mae also wanted to inspire young people. She began helping teachers and students learn science in new ways. She wrote four science books for kids. She also became a college **professor**.

In 2012, Mae applied to NASA again. She wanted to join a project called 100 Year Starship. NASA picked Mae to lead it. She was excited. Her team studies how to travel to distant stars within 100 years.

Mae still dreams big dreams. She inspires big dreams in others, too!

TIME LINE

1956: Mae Carol Jemison is born in Decatur, Alabama, on October 17.

1959: Mae's family moves to Chicago. It becomes Mae's hometown.

1968: Mae goes to high school at age 12.

1972: Mae wins a scholarship to go to Stanford University at age 16.

1977: Mae graduates from Stanford. She enters Cornell University Medical School to become a doctor.

1980: Mae volunteers at a refugee camp in Asia.

1981: Mae graduates from Cornell and becomes a doctor in California.

1983–1985: Mae volunteers in Africa as a doctor in the Peace Corps.

1985: Mae applies to NASA astronaut training for the first time.

1986: The space shuttle Challenger explodes on January 28. NASA stops training astronauts.

1987: NASA starts training astronauts again. Mae applies for the second time. She is accepted as the first African-American woman.

1992: Mae and the Endeavour crew blast off to space on September 12. They are in space for eight days.

1993: Mae is the first astronaut to be a guest on *Star Trek*.

1993: Mae leaves NASA to start her company, The Jemison Group. It brings technology to places in need.

1994: Mae starts a foundation named after her mother. It hosts a teen science camp and works with teachers.

1995: Mae becomes a professor at Dartmouth College.

2012: Mae returns to NASA to lead 100 Year Starship.

GLOSSARY

applied (uh-PLYED): asked for officially

engineer (en-juh-NEER): someone trained to design and build things

experiments (ik-SPER-uh-ments): tests to try out how things work

gravity (GRAV-i-tee): the force that pulls things toward the center of Earth and keeps them from floating away

planetarium (plan-i-TAIR-ee-uhm): a building where the positions of planets, moons, and stars are projected onto a curved ceiling

professor (pruh-FES-ur): a teacher at a college or university

technology (tek-NAH-luh-jee): machines and equipment developed through science and engineering

volunteered (vah-luhn-TEERD): offered to do a job without pay

INDEX

TEXT-DEPENDENT QUESTIONS

1. What did Mae Jemison like to do as a child?

2. What show did Mae like to watch?

3. Where did Mae volunteer as a doctor?

4. When did Mae go to space?

5. How has Mae shared her life with others?

EXTENSION ACTIVITY

Pick a woman you know who has made a difference in people's lives. It might be someone in your family or community. Interview her. What were her childhood dreams? What did she do to follow them? What was hard? What inspired her? Write this woman's story. Include how she inspires you to follow your own dreams.

ABOUT THE AUTHOR

Meeg Pincus loves to write about "solutionaries"—real people who help solve problems for people, animals, and the planet. She also loves to teach kids how they can be solutionaries, too. (Yes, every kid can!) Learn more about Meeg, her books, and solutionary education at www.MeegPincus.com.

ABOUT THE ILLUSTRATOR

Elena Bia was born in a little town in northern Italy, near the Alps. In her free time, she puts her heart into personal comics. She also loves walking on the beach and walking through the woods. For her, flowers are the most beautiful form of life.

www.rourkebooks.com

Quote sources: "Mae Jemison", Physicians, Changing the Face of Medicine (website), https://cfmedicine.nlm.nih.gov/physicians/biography_168.html; "The Secret Lives of Scientists and Engineers", Mae Jemison, interview by NOVA, PBS, July 31, 2014, video, https://www.pbs.org/wgbh/nova/article/the-secret-life-of-scientists-and-engineers-mae-jemison/

PHOTO CREDIT: Page 20: ©Wiki

Edited by: Kim Thompson
Illustrated by: Elena Bia
Cover and interior layout by: Rhea Magaro-Wallace

Library of Congress PCN Data

Mae C. Jemison / Meeg Pincus
 (Women in Science and Technology)
  ISBN 978-1-73161-428-5 (hard cover)
  ISBN 978-1-73161-223-6 (soft cover)
  ISBN 978-1-73161-533-6 (e-Book)
  ISBN 978-1-73161-638-8 (ePub)
Library of Congress Control Number: 2019932134

Rourke Educational Media
Printed in the United States of America
02-3152211937